Violet

Manasvini Duggal

BookLeaf Publishing

Presentation by *BookLeaf Publishing*

Web: www.bookleafpub.com

E-mail: info@bookleafpub.com

ISBN: 9789357219839

First edition 2023

ACKNOWLEDGEMENT

I would like to start by thanking my family- my mother, father, and aunt for constantly urging me to write and exhibit my work. From helping me create and maintain my first blog, to constantly supporting the publication of my first book, they have been very important to my foundation as a writer. Secondly, thanks to everyone on the BookLeaf Publishing team, without whom it would not have been possible to publish this collection. Lastly, I would like to highlight the continued love and understanding that comes from my closest friends, those in Delhi as well as Dublin. From reading every single piece I have ever written to helping me publish my first book, I know they will be my support for every written word, published or unpublished, that is yet to come.

Lavender

Let the sunshine through
a grey-blue pall,
the winter lets out a dismal call
and I see a red moon burn through
a naked glass floor;
someday, I think,
I'm going to live where the stars fall close
where the city sounds stray near
an incandescent shore,
and venus shines through a speck in the clouds.

Someday, I think,
I'd like to live above where
the Aegean meets its blue
and a god rises true out of the lavender sky.
maybe I'll see him burn blue,
through a naked cellar floor.

Nordic Sky

Emotions, love,
run as redundant as the breeze
in the nordic night sky,
run as cold as the frost
that crystallises across the glass;
the glass that I gaze out of
onto fields of white and blue.

orange, pink and pale
run the chemtrails that trail behind
the sapphic colours of the nordic sky.
orange, pink and sapphire
comes the golden nordic dusk.

I can dream again,
I can fly.
I can feel time freeze
with every elevation I touch;

Colourless crystals suddenly breathe
pink
into the nordic sky.
After so long, I breathe the same.

Starry-Eyed

Fragility, I surpass.
Good deeds for you,
I have none.

You always thought me the best of you,
yet you never considered the heavens
I would have to move
to get you past the rotting helm
of your own dying star;

now my love for you shadows
beneath sapphires burnt into the night sky;
the heavens reflected,
starry-eyed,
onto the world I have beyond your hold

Flight AY122

I woke up to the gauze of butterflies
flying between my ribcage
and lungs;
I could feel them glow pink
and white and blue
on the day that I flew
against the colours
of a sapphic northern sky,

against a window crystallised pink
under the setting horizon's light,
over where I was allowed to be alone;

how I missed being alone.

and with rolling clouds to my left,
violet fields to my right,
I live to be in the hold of the fruition
I am in now;

and for that, I am grateful.

Lilies in Rome

i. I see a future,
a summer in a novella under Rome.
A glimpse of pears and lilies,
and clementines and a rose,
a picture holding your smile's very soul,
and a molten breeze
across a blueberry sky.

ii. I picture venus;
my love for you a lark in the sky,
and I see her shine through my dress
and its crimson folds.
In the eyes of a sun-wed dreamer
you sparkle and shine.
In my eyes, *you remain.*
In you, I am no longer enshrined.

iii. I picture worse but all I fear is being alone,
in reality, I read James Joyce
and all I understand is remorse.
you beckon, come closer,
but its someone else to bring back home;
in her arms, you'll find yourself in Rome.

In her eyes, you catch your breath.
In my thoughts, all I catch is you.

Amethyst

I never quite believed
in the magics that come
trapped within the hardened molecules of stone.
I never quite believed
in any powers beyond the unknown;
I never believed and yet,
I bought myself an amethyst anyway.

 I never quite considered
that maybe angels, so cosmic,
do not speak to us outright.
I always thought I was special enough
to be foretold.
I never considered that fates
and the future
came not from destiny, but from a hardened
soul.

I hung my amethyst on a chain of gold,
and now I watch it dip daylight through
a purple rose;

I never went looking for magic then.
Now, I find some everyday.

Prayer // New York

In the face of a dead-end cold,
in the rot of a hellish peak
and the seasons that come to follow
the ends of a setting earth,

I never thought I'd see the sun
rise in a lavender so bright.

I never thought I'd face a celestial
in the dewdrop down a periwinkle's back.

I never thought I'd find a future so enticing
in the broken, red bricks of new york.

I never thought I'd have the gall
to find it alone.

Magdalene

Maybe she's my full moon,
maybe she's an oasis full of respite,
or maybe,
the glowering edge of a bullet down my spine.
Maybe she is a sprite
born of an anti-God,
the donatella of an antichrist.
maybe she's saccharine, a primadonna,

kisses soft as primavera;

who were you running from,
did they forgive you?

my Madonna,
Magdalena.

Romeo and Juliet

If I ever wrote a story on love,
I would want it to be a happy one;
too many within reality
seem to forget
how a meeting of souls should really end,
how a collision of bones can send
a shooting star across the acres of a burning sky.

I always succumb to the feeling I felt for you,
for you were my favourite time of day

And if I ever wrote a song of love,
I wouldn't want it to be like the Dire Straits one;
too many within rock 'n' roll
seem to know better than most what it feels like
to wish upon a cold,
unresponsive field of stars.

I always sang along with the skies above, now,
I never wish I would again

Fidelity

I am finding remorse on my own two feet,
I can light up the morose
in a way I could not
three hundred and seventy-five days ago.
I am finding fidelity in my own four limbs
I can find comfort
in my own body and bones,

and I can feel a spine
strong and starlit inside;
it has inlays of violet and gold.

and with a breath the colour of a setting star,
I find my joy in being free of love.

Loving Memory

i. I wrote once
about a fairytale at home,
and a love I swore was never forlorn,
and a depiction of a future I thought was
sublime. I wrote once,
about how youth rarely bears the luxury
of things that last through time.
I wrote of all these things,
and now, months later,
only one of these holds true.

ii. Every generation of love
seems to bear the mark of its time;
I think ours stands cold in the caustic rain,
writing letters to a God who did not stay to see
us ordained.
ii.i And now, everything I touch slips away like
dew.
    Nothing paints the sky like love-
    true blue.
    In youthful,
    loving memory,
    I will think of you.

iii. Just as I am, I write,
I hope I stay.

Saint Vixen

Who am I
but the world to you?
I am the pink in your moonlight,
The sparkle of sun
in your December grey,
and all the beauty Byron wrote about;
I am all there is,
until I am nothing.

Then what am I?

I am Magdalena,
I am your Antichrist.
Saint Vixen.
Primadonna.
A sacrilege, a cheat; *I am vice*
I glow pink in my own room,
blossoming alone.
Without any of you,
I am violet, gold and daylight

Over,
and over,
and again.

Sapphic

Tell me your childhood secrets,
show me your favourite moles;
your eyes overflow
with the love you wear all over your soul.

I often think of the sunlight you braid
into your curls from time to time

Turn the light on,
it's a new kind of bright;
your friendship and mine
held together in a shared lovers' twine.

I think of your laughter,
I can hear it shimmer inside

In rain or moonlight,
we simmer.
I would dance with you till the end of the night;
and in our little way, I know you would too

Ada

I find your eyes speckled, and in them,
I see a spider hanging low on her crystalline
web.
Dotted black in a translucent hole,
even your soul can't bare through your retinas,
your love won't drip out of your lobes.
And your liver is a shred of remorse, I heard,
and resentment only ever glazes your bones.
Spite set its hold on your spine,
and its home in your heart of gold.

I never understood the word 'lover' before you,
I'll never feel the mask of desolation anytime
after.

I'll never see a black widow
dancing against a naked soul
ever again.

Long Live

Thank you for the hope you'd bring,
for the crevices in the night
where I would have to think
and write and abscond
in ways I never knew how to before I was
seventeen years old;

I took you then,
and I turned you into a piece of my soul.

And even if you never know
quite where to look and see,
I will still keep you in my thoughts,
between the words of my book
and rose-scented tea.
I will let you die some other night, but for now,

I let you live another day.

Monks on Mange St.

Monks from a street of mange
pass by
my single alleyed route;
I join them for an hour,
come back to the silence of my room.

Somehow, I feel their pain
more ardently than they do,
somehow I feel their malady
in 5 shades of gold.

sorrow, and its waves, come crash
with a scent of faintly fragrant lilies.

all my senses, in empathy,

they flicker.

And maybe, if I didn't see a world
beyond this hold,
if I didn't mould my senses to try and afford
to be a seamstress to the stars;
maybe then I'd also see myself
in the many faces of art.

Somehow, everyone else sees my pain
more plainly than I do,
but only I paint the scene
in 7 shades of violet and rose.

daylight and its wallows, come creeping
inside my melodies.

my body and bones, they sing

for that golden street of mange.

Cosmos

i. Maybe there is to come a time
where in vermillion plains we might find
the shattered cosmos of a god.
In those skies warring with skies,
we might approach infinity
in a space no further than our known;
infinity, that is dark, cold
and neon.

ii. In the eyes of a Bombay dreamer,
I saw Venus reflected in the clouds,
I saw Jupiter shine through the shrouds
of an intangible atmospheric night;
I think that the universe
cannot be captured
in complicated equational math.
I think sometimes, someone's smile might be
enough.

iii. I hope the universe reflects the colours
of purple orchids and opalite stone;
I hope that infinity stretches brighter,
and farther,
than the gifts we have in our known;
than what our minds are meant to understand.

I know our cosmos is forever out of our reach,
I hope that is the way it stays.

Sea Foam

The days are disappointing when I miss you.
When the white foam seas are gone and all in
their place,
a hushed grey fume.
I wish you were close to my chest where I could
rest my head
on yours,
and we could feel our love in our bones.

I wish you were home with me, by the comfort
of sea light.

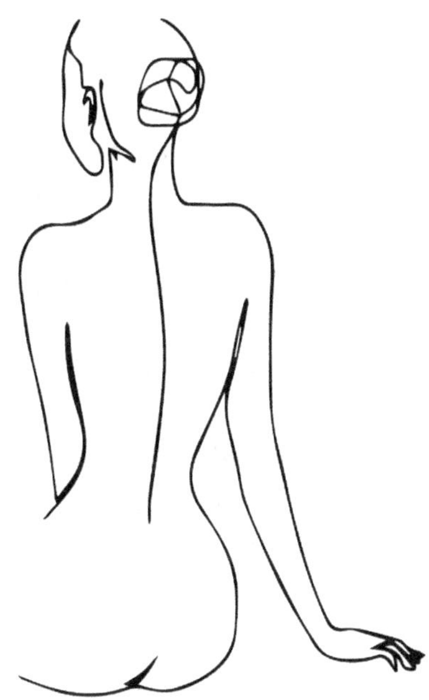

Art

Paint for this scene a modest gold.
with strands the colour of a burnt-out flame,
I had to ask the stars for a final refrain,
but a collection of fires and ages have never
known anything less
and rarely ever more.
And with words spun out on repeat,
I wished the ones before a kinder sea,
as I counted up kisses to build a dream on.
But,
for all my trysts with artistry,
for all the chords I have struck and the
paintbrushes I amateurly wield,
I always needed the universe to tell me what I
felt lost for;
I wish the stars had told me then and before,
to follow true north away,
to a gallery of broken hearts,
to a crescendo of murmured scores;

until all I saw in the horizon was art.

And with music and love,
came hope and grace;
from sapling verses

to words bound in faith,
I find answers in love, in lovers wrapped in
moonlight,
in dancing alone as the music turns to wine,

and in the distance, dotted with sunset-driven
stars;
all I see in the horizon is art.

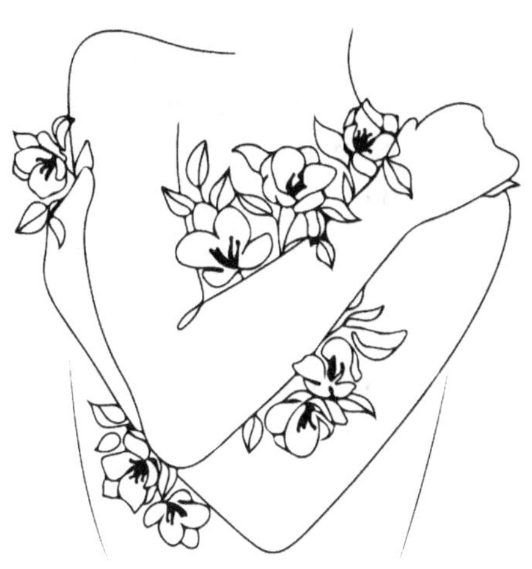

Moonstone

Just like us, do the waters dream
of a world beyond the hollows that we know?
Would they sing a song for an evening star,
for a light borne unto cosmic tar;
if an ocean were to make music,
would it sound like love,
or remorse?

And just like that, would the crashing waves
be the envy of a worldly sky?
Would a starry night crave to exist
beyond the soundless ebony
on which it is enshrined;
would the moonlight feel beautiful,
or hoarse?

Would we still matter,
if the universe decided to elope?

Faith Healer: II

i. I have thought of gods and ghosts,
I have thought of celestial stones
and their artificial ruse;
I have thought of burning hearth and home,
in the carnage of break and bone, and in all of it, I
have heard back from no one but myself.

ii. I have written on silver pennies and to
maleficent skies;
I have written on the wings of sparrows,
and not one has written back,
except in silver linings on the occasional cloud.
I saw those then, and for them I am grateful.

iii. I drove all night for questions I don't remember,
and now
I have no doubt that the universe herself
gives out little doses of faith healers.
Lately, I do not pretend to have all the answers,
I do not bother the cosmos for signs and rejected
calls
for lately, it has come to my attention,

I am just twenty years old,
and there is so much living left to do.